A MIDSUMMER NIGHT'S DREAM
or
The Night They Missed the Forest for the Trees

Adapted from Shakespeare's Play

by

NANCY LINEHAN CHARLES

Dramatic Publishing
Woodstock, Illinois • England • Australia • New Zealand

8

A MIDSUMMER NIGHT'S DREAM
or
The Night They Missed the Forest for the Trees

A Full-length Play

For 4 Men and 6 Women, 9 either, extras

<u>Three Storytellers</u>:
  Jessie/Theseus
  Kaytlin/Hippolyta
  Anna/Egeus

<u>Four Teenagers</u>:
  Hermia
  Lysander
  Helena
  Demetrius

<u>Six Rude Mechanicals</u>:
  Peter Quince
  Nick Bottom, the weaver
  Francis Flute, the bellows mender
  Tom Snout, the tinker
  Snug, the joiner
  Robin Starveling, the tailor

<u>Forest Folk</u>:
  Oberon, King of the Fairies
  Titania, Queen of the Fairies
  Robin Goodfellow (Puck), mischievous servant to Oberon
  Fairies attending on Titania:
    Peaseblossom
    Cobweb
    Mustardseed
    Mote

Many forest fairies who can also double as lords and ladies in the court of Theseus.

NOTE: The three storytellers must be girls, the four teens are gender-specific, as are Titania (f) and Oberon (m). Bottom needs to be male. All other roles will accommodate either gender.

Set requirements: Bare stage with set pieces moved on for palace plants or ropes for trees in the forest.

Approximate running time: 1 hour

A MIDSUMMER NIGHT'S DREAM
or
The Night They Missed the Forest for the Trees

SCENE: *A dark stage. Ideally, ropes hang from the grid, down to a foot or two above the floor. They have ivy wound around them. At various intervals, there are also strips of green material, hanging between the ropes. This is the forest where most of the action takes place. Trees in pots can fill in the space. This would be nice, but depending on your budget, and your grid...use your imagination.*

AT RISE: *Lights pop up on fifteen to twenty kids, in various positions with books in front of them on the floor. All are snoozing. This is study hall.*

V.O. (JESSIE)
Teenagers.

   (The STORYTELLER walks into the light.)

JESSIE
Ya can't live with 'em; ya can't live without 'em.
But sometimes...they're like a bad dream

(One of the boys wakes up, runs his hand over his mouth ... raises his shirt slowly to wipe his face ... revealing a large, hideous tattoo.)

JESSIE
See what I mean?

KAYTLIN
It gets tedious, doesn't it? Adult says no ... kid says ...

ALL KIDS *(waking suddenly, defiantly slapping the floor in unison)*
YES!!!

KAYTLIN
Never mind the subject.

JESSIE
You've planted a radish, and suddenly, around thirteen, you've got a kumquat ... an ORNERY kumquat ...

ANNA
And this is nothing new. It's been going on for hundreds and hundreds of years.

KAYTLIN
William Shakespeare knew all about teenagers ... *and* their dreams.

JESSIE
Some things never change. *(She looks around.)* Now ... this is study hall.

(And one by one ... in very quick succession ... heads flop forward onto the floor ... with a nice, loud THWACK ... and

they are all asleep. JESSIE walks slowly around, looking at these drowsy sluggards.)

JESSIE

I mean, look at 'em. They have a test tomorrow on the very play Will Shakespeare wrote about them: *Midsummer Night's Dream.* And what are they doing? Dreaming!

(She clears her throat loudly. The teens wake up and, thinking perhaps an adult is present, they pretend they're busy. They sit up straight. They each are reading a book which they mime in front of them. Slowly they all sink into the following positions: One or two go back to sleep and drool on their books. One boy throws paper airplanes across the room at a girl. Two are in a very close and seemingly intimate conversation. JESSIE and two other girls, ANNA and KAYTLIN, sit in a circle gossiping. Another boy, DEMETRIUS, stares longingly at HERMIA talking intimately to LYSANDER. And another girl, HELENA, stares at DEMETRIUS. Six well-meaning—but maybe "not-playing-with-all-jets-on-burn"— boys sit toward the back, looking innocent and expectant, with slide rules and such hanging off their belts— the RUDE MECHANICALS. The captain of the football team and the head cheerleader, OBERON and TITANIA, have their backs to each other, arms folded across their chests in a seething, argumentative position. And the arty crowd—berets and leather—sits looking bored [FAIRIES]. The class clown, PUCK, juggles at his desk...or perhaps launches a pea-shooter assault.)

JESSIE
Look, I know I'm bossy ...

ALL STUDENTS *(turning ... in perfect unison)*
Nah, not you, Jessie.

> *(JESSIE whips her head around to glare at them ... and
> they return to their positions.)*

JESSIE *(continuing her thread)*
... but the idea just seemed obvious. I knew the play.
And I knew I was probably the only one who DID!!!

> *(A groan from the kids.)*

So I could run the whole show. An idea close to my heart.
I mean, we had all the characters: Ever see four more obvious teenagers than these?

> *(She indicates LYSANDER and HERMIA, smitten with each
> other; then DEMETRIUS, looking ga-ga over HERMIA,
> and HELENA weeping over DEMETRIUS.)*

JESSIE *(turning to another storyteller)*
Am I right?

ANNA
Always, Jessie, always.
And the Rude Mechanicals—those are the
sorta dopey crew in *Midsummer Night's Dream*—tailors
and tinkers and so forth—who want to do a play for Duke
Theseus' wedding. How 'bout ... these guys?

(She indicates six kids, looking like they haven't a clue.)

KAYTLIN
Perfect!!! Well-meaning and goofy. That's a compliment, guys.

(The RUDE MECHANICALS smile appreciatively...but with low wattage.)

ANNA
And the King and Queen of the Forest where
the Dream takes place—Oberon and Titania.
Well, who else but the oh-so-popular football captain
and the head cheerleader???

JESSIE
Now you're cookin'. And then there's a character named
Puck. Plays practical jokes on people. Sorta the class clown.

(She grabs PUCK up by the shirt. He points to her waist.)

PUCK
Hey, Jess. What's that?

(JESSIE looks down. He brings his hand up and flicks her in the nose. She rolls her eyes.)

JESSIE *(to the audience)*
Am I right or am I right?
Sit down, clown.

(PUCK sits, chortling to himself, à la Jimmy Durante.)

PUCK
I got a million of 'em.

KAYTLIN
And we've seen 'em all, buddy.
Puck is joined in the forest
by a zillion spirits—fairies and wood sprites—who hang
with Titania, the Queen of the Forest. That could be
these guys.

(She points to the arty crowd.)

ARTY GUY (MUSTARDSEED)
Do we have lines?

KAYTLIN
A few.

ARTY GIRL (COBWEB)
We're artists, ya know.

KAYTLIN *(to JESSIE, as though things are unraveling)*
The actors are counting their lines.

ANOTHER ARTY GUY (PEASEBLOSSOM)
(sullenly aggressive)
Do we deliver the social and moral message of the piece?

JESSIE
You get to wear beautiful painted costumes.

ARTY GUY (MUSTARDSEED)
Cool.

ARTY GIRL (COBWEB)
Okay.

ANOTHER ARTY GUY (PEASEBLOSSOM)
Deal.

JESSIE *(to the audience)*
Ya can't just be a producer anymore.
Ya gotta be a diplomat.
(looking at ANNA and KAYTLIN)
So what's left?

KAYTLIN & ANNA
The grownups.

ALL THREE STORYTELLERS
Ooooooooooo.

JESSIE
Tell ya what. Let's us play them. *(To the audience.)*
'Cause, ya see...there are basically three grownups in this
play. And basically three of us. Fits like a glove.

KAYTLIN
Yeah, there's Egeus, father of this teenager, Hermia.
You do that, Anna.

ANNA
I'm a girl.

JESSIE & KAYTLIN *(staring at her)*
Duuuhhh!!!

JESSIE
Loosen up, will ya. It's the millennium cross-gender thing.

ANNA
Oh.

JESSIE
Just talk in a deep voice like a father. And act like you
have a lot of opinions but are essentially clueless.

ANNA
Yeah, I got that.

JESSIE *(to the audience)*
There aren't any mothers in this play or we'd make one
of you Dads play it. We take no prisoners.

KAYTLIN
So, Jess. You and I will play Duke Theseus and his about-
to-be wife Hippolyta, right?

JESSIE
Right. I'll do the girl.

ANNA
What happened to the millennium cross-gender thing?

JESSIE
Alright, alright. I'll play Duke Theseus. *(emphatically)* And
I'll play him *well*.

KAYTLIN
Are we ready?

JESSIE
Yep. Places, everyone!!!

(JESSIE and KAYTLIN, as THESEUS and HIPPOLYTA, sit facing the audience. All the other players sit around the edge.)

JESSIE
Alright, I'm about to become Theseus now: Duke of Athens. And Kaytlin here is my fiancée, Hippolyta. We'll change hats...so you'll know.

(KAYTLIN turns her storyteller hat to her HIPPOLYTA hat.)

JESSIE
And just as we're getting ready to celebrate and get married, in comes this annoying father, dragging his teenage daughter behind him. You remember about teenagers, don't'cha? Mind of their own?

(JESSIE turns her storyteller hat to her THESEUS hat.)

ANNA *(as EGEUS)*
Full of vexation come I, with complaint
Against my child, my daughter Hermia.
Stand forth, Demetrius. My noble lord,
This man hath my consent to marry her.
Stand forth, Lysander.
This man hath bewitched my child
by moonlight, with rings, trifles, sweetmeats.
Turned her obedience
To stubborn harshness.
If she will not here before your Grace

Consent to marry with Demetrius,
I beg the ancient privilege of Athens:
As she is mine, I may dispose of her,
Which shall be either to this gentleman ...
(He points to DEMETRIUS.)
... Or to her death according to our law.

(JESSIE turns the THESEUS hat around to her story-teller hat.)

JESSIE
Now that's harsh!!!! Do you believe that? If you disobeyed
your dad, you could be killed ... legally!!!!!

(She turns THESEUS hat back around.)

JESSIE *(as THESEUS)*
What say you, Hermia?
Demetrius is a worthy gentleman.

HERMIA
So is Lysander.
I would my father looked but with my eyes.
I do entreat your Grace to pardon me.
But what is the worst that may befall me
If I refuse to wed Demetrius.

JESSIE *(as THESEUS)*
Either to die the death, or to abjure
Forever the society of men.
Therefore, fair Hermia, question your desires.

HERMIA
So will I die, my lord.

JESSIE *(as THESEUS)*
Take time to pause, and by the next new moon,
Upon that day either prepare to die
For disobedience to your father's will,
Or else to wed Demetrius.

DEMETRIUS
Relent, sweet Hermia, and, Lysander, yield
Thy craz-ed title to my certain right.

LYSANDER
You have her father's love, Demetrius.
Marry him.
I am beloved of beauteous Hermia.
(To THESEUS.)
Demetrius made love to Helena
And won her soul; and she, sweet lady, dotes ...

   (From the side, HELENA lurches forward ... SOOO EMBAR-
   RASSED ... she can only look at all assembled ... and col-
   lapse in a terrible wail ...)

HELENA
Oooooooooooooooooooohhhhhh!!!!!!!

LYSANDER
... Upon this spotted and inconstant man.

JESSIE *(as THESEUS, with finality)*
I have heard so much.
For you, fair Hermia, look you arm yourself

To fit your fancies to your father's will.
Or else the law of Athens yields you up
To death or to a vow of single life.

(The COURT leaves, and the STORYTELLERS turn their hats to the storytelling side.)

JESSIE
Well, that'd curl your hair, wouldn't it?
What a bunch'a choices: marry a guy who makes
you want to swallow glass...become a nun...or die.
Hot diggety!!!!!!

ANNA
Still...teenagers can squirm out of almost anything. Watch.

LYSANDER
How now, my love? Why is your cheek so pale?

(HERMIA has a severe pout-on.)

LYSANDER
Ay me! The course of true love never did run smooth.

HERMIA *(stamps her foot)*
Oh hell! To choose love by another's eyes!

KAYTLIN
Watch your language, kid. We wanna keep a G-rating.

LYSANDER *(suddenly has an idea, excitedly)*
I have a widow aunt from Athens—her house remote
seven leagues.

And she respects me as her only son.
There, gentle Hermia, may I marry thee.

(Pout gone ... HERMIA turns with a BIG smile.)

JESSIE
So much for Dad's wishes. She's
outta there!!!!!

LYSANDER
If thou lovest me, then
Steal forth thy father's house tomorrow night,
And in the wood,
There will I stay for thee.

HERMIA
By all the vows that ever men have broke
(In number more than ever women spoke),
Tomorrow truly will I meet with thee.

KAYTLIN
Boy, they're gonna be so busted!!!!

(Enter HELENA, droopy and sniffling.)

HELENA *(to HERMIA)*
O, teach me how you look and with what art
You sway the motion of Demetrius' heart!

HERMIA
The more I hate, the more he follows me.

HELENA
The more I love, the more he hateth me.

HERMIA
Take comfort: he no more shall see my face.
Lysander and myself will fly this place.

LYSANDER
Tomorrow night...through Athens' gates have we devised
to steal.

HERMIA
And in the wood...Lysander and myself shall meet...
and thence from Athens.
Farewell, sweet playfellow. Pray thou for us,
And good luck grant thee thy Demetrius.

*(LYSANDER and HERMIA run off opposite sides of the
stage, blowing kisses to each other as they go...and it is
REALLY gooey. HELENA watches, looking droopy.)*

ANNA
Just what you need to see when you're in a bad mood.
Two teenagers in looooove. Yuch!!!

*(HELENA watches, seething and sad. Then turns to the
audience.)*

HELENA
How happy some o'er other some can be!!!
Through Athens I am thought as fair as she.
But what of that? Demetrius thinks not so.
(She gets a devilish look on her face.)
I will go tell him of fair Hermia's flight.
Then to the wood will he tomorrow night
Pursue her.

(She rubs her hands together in anticipation.)
Herein mean I to enrich my pain.
To have his sight thither and back again.

(She runs off. JESSIE comes to the edge of the stage. She points a finger at the audience.)

JESSIE
Ever liked someone who didn't like you?
Agony!!
And chasing after them usually doesn't get
you very far.

KAYTLIN
But I guess Helena doesn't have anyone to tell her that.
Oh, that's right. She's a teenager.
She wouldn't listen anyway.

ANNA
So, Hermia and Lysander are running away to get
married. Helena is going to tell that secret
to Demetrius, hoping he'll be so mad, he'll
get over Hermia.

JESSIE
Don't count on it. Shakespeare's got some fun up
his sleeve. All four teenagers will end up in that wood.
And then ... look out!

ANNA
Meanwhile, everyone else is excited about Duke
Theseus and Hippolyta's wedding ...

KAYTLIN
... mostly because it's gonna be like a holiday ... or a Teacher-in-Service Day ... everybody gets to sleep late.

(A crash backstage and the RUDE MECHANICALS wander on confused by the backstage chaos. Each has a tool in his/her hand and these even seem to baffle this goofy crew.)

JESSIE
So a bunch of kinda dopey, good-natured fellows decide they're gonna put on a play for the Duke. Peter Quince, the director, is in a casting session.

QUINCE
Is all our company here?

(One blows his nose loudly, one burps, one lies down and snores. His mates pick him up and hold him upright.)

ANNA
They're short on experienced actors in Athens.

BOTTOM
First, good Peter Quince, say what the play
treats on, then read the names of the actors.

QUINCE
Our play is "The Most Lamentable Comedy,
and Most Cruel Death of Pyramus and Thisbe."
(Note: pronounced Pier-uh-muss and Thiz-bee.)

JESSIE
Comedy and Death in the same play?
This should be interesting.

QUINCE
Answer as I call you. Nick Bottom, the weaver.

BOTTOM *(stands forth dramatically)*
Ready. Name what part I am for.

QUINCE
You, Nick Bottom, are set down for Pyramus...
a lover that kills himself most gallant for love.

BOTTOM
That will ask some tears in the true performing of it.
Let the audience look to their eyes.
I will move storms.
(dramatically)
The raging rocks
And shivering shocks
Shall break the locks...
This was lofty.

QUINCE *(interrupting)*
Francis Flute, the bellows mender. You
must take Thisbe on you.

FLUTE *(not the sharpest tool in the shed)*
What is Thisbe...a wandering knight?

QUINCE
It is the lady Pyramus must love.

FLUTE
Nay, faith, let not me play a woman.

ANNA *(with a look to JESSIE)*
Apparently hasn't heard of the millennium
cross-gender thing.

JESSIE
Wrong century.
Although ... it might enlighten
you to know that in Shakespeare's day, men played
all the women's parts.

ANNA *(defensively)*
I knew that.
I was just testing.

FLUTE
I have a beard coming.

KAYTLIN
In your dreams.

BOTTOM *(excitedly)*
Let me play Thisbe too!!!
I'll speak in a monstrous little voice:
(squeaking)
"Ah, Pyramus, my lover dear."

QUINCE
NO!!!

JESSIE
I love a strong director.

QUINCE *(becoming irritated)*
Robin Starveling... you must play Thisbe's mother.
Tom Snout, the tinker... you, Pyramus' father.
Myself Thisbe's father.

(BOTTOM starts to interrupt, QUINCE overrides him.)

QUINCE
Snug, the joiner... you the lion's part.

SNUG
Have you the lion's part written? If so, give it me.
For I am slow of study.

QUINCE *(stares at him)*
It is nothing but roaring.

BOTTOM *(erupting)*
Let me play the lion too.

JESSIE
What a greedy guts. He wants to play all the parts.

BOTTOM
I will roar that I will do any man's heart good to hear me.
The Duke will say "Let him roar again!!"

QUINCE *(trying to maintain order)*
You should do it too terribly, you would
fright the Duchess, and that were enough to hang us all.

ALL *(nodding in agreement)*
That would hang us, every mother's son.

BOTTOM *(pushing harder)*
But I will aggravate my voice so that I will
roar you as gently as any nightingale.

(BOTTOM lets forth with a few gurgling roars. QUINCE loses it.)

QUINCE
YOU CAN PLAY NO PART BUT PYRAMUS!!!!!!

ANNA
That's tellin' him.

QUINCE
Masters, here are your parts. Tomorrow night,
meet me in the palace wood, a mile without the town,
by moonlight. There will we rehearse.

BOTTOM *(so excited)*
We may rehearse most obscenely and courageously.
Take pains. Be perfect. Adieu.

(The RUDE MECHANICALS wander off in different directions, studying their parts. JESSIE comes forward.)

JESSIE
We're gettin' a full house here, headin' for the forest. So
far we got four runaway teenagers, and six
goofs all convening in a very tiny woods.

KAYTLIN
Who's next?

(From the sides of the stage, through the trees comes a slew of FAIRIES, dancing and tumbling around the stage. They each carry a tiny pinspot flashlight. They flick them on and off. PUCK comes from offstage, bounding to center.)

JESSIE
OK, here we have the arty crowd from study hall. Remember? The ones who wanted more lines? And also ...

(PUCK comes up to her and extends his hand ... clenched in a fist ... and says "Hit that." She does ... and his hand swings around ... his arm fully extended ... like Curly of the Stooges ... and bonks her on the head ... he withdraws ... satisfied ... with a Nyuk ... Nyuk ... Nyuk ... chuckle.)

JESSIE *(recovering)*
... yeah. The class clown. He plays Robin Goodfellow. More commonly known as Puck. He serves the King of the Fairies ... Oberon.

KAYTLIN *(to the audience)*
Say that after me: Oh-burr-ahn.

(Audience follows suit. The FAIRIES fly and dance all over the stage. Anyone with gymnastics training would be good for these parts.)

PUCK
How now, spirit. Whither wander you?

MUSTARDSEED
Our queen and all her elves come here anon.

ANNA
The Queen of the Fairies is Titania. Come on, you know the routine. Repeat after me: ti-tahn-ya.

(Audience does so.)

PUCK
The KING doth keep his revels here tonight.
Take heed the Queen come not within his sight.

JESSIE
OK. Plot point here. Oberon and Titania are having a fight. And they're both acting like children.

ANNA
Which is only slightly better than acting like teenagers.

KAYTLIN
See, Titania has a new little boy in her court. They call him a changeling boy.

JESSIE
Don't ask.

ANNA
And Oberon's just jealous because Titania's paying so much attention to this boy.

PUCK
But room, Fairy. Here comes Oberon.

MUSTARDSEED
And here my mistress. Would that he were gone!

(Enter TITANIA and OBERON from opposite sides of the stage—both looking haughtily at each other—both with retinues of FAIRIES. Read: as many as you'd like to cast.)

JESSIE
Uh-oh. Here comes trouble.

OBERON *(through his clenched teeth)*
Ill met by moonlight, proud Titania.

TITANIA *(taunting)*
What, jealous Oberon?

OBERON
Why should Titania cross her Oberon?
I but beg a little changeling boy.

TITANIA *(angry)*
His mother was a votress of my order,
And for her sake do I rear up the boy,
And for her sake, I will not part with him.

OBERON *(also angry)*
How long within this wood intend you stay?

TITANIA *(defiant)*
Perchance 'til after Theseus' wedding day.
(more subdued now)
Go with us.

OBERON
Give me that boy and I will go with thee.

TITANIA
Not for thy fairy kingdom! Fairies, away!!
We shall chide outright, if I longer stay.

OBERON *(shouting)*
Well, go thy way!

KAYTLIN
Now you may think it's strange for people to be talking
about who OWNS a boy. But these are fairies ... otherworldly
folks ... and I guess have a kind of ... different culture.

ANNA
Anyway, Oberon's fuming because he can't have his own
way. Big spoiled brat. And he wants revenge. So he calls
on the class clown!!!

OBERON
My gentle Puck, come hither.
Fetch me that flower; the herb I showed thee once.
The juice of it on sleeping eyelids laid
Will make a man or woman madly dote
Upon the next live creature that it sees.
Fetch me this herb!

PUCK
I'll put a girdle round the earth
In forty minutes!

JESSIE
Bet he's got a ton of frequent-flyer miles.

(PUCK flies off stage.)

OBERON
Having once this juice,
I'll watch Titania when she is asleep
And drop the liquor of it in her eyes.
The next thing that she, waking, looks upon
(Be it lion, bear, or wolf or bull
or meddling monkey or busy ape)
She shall pursue it with the soul of love.
And ere I take this charm from off her sight
(As I can take it with another herb)
I'll make her render up her boy to me.
But who comes here?
(He makes a gesture around himself and you hear the tinkle of bells.)
I am invisible,
And I will overhear their conference.

(Enter HELENA and DEMETRIUS...she...hot on his heels. During the following, OBERON moves about the TEENS freely, since they can't see him.)

KAYTLIN
The TEENS have arrived! The teens have arrived! Welcome to the woods, guys.

DEMETRIUS *(turning on HELENA)*
I love thee not; therefore, pursue me not!
Where is Lysander and fair Hermia?
Get thee gone and follow me no more!

HELENA *(groaning)*
You draw me, you hard-hearted adamant!!

DEMETRIUS
Do I speak you fair?
Rather do I not, in plainest truth
Tell you I do not, nor I cannot love you?

HELENA
And even for that do I love you the more.

JESSIE
Poor girl!!!

HELENA
I am your spaniel and, Demetrius,
The more you beat me I will fawn on you.
Give me leave, unworthy as I am, to follow you.

JESSIE
No, no, no, Helena ... !!!
You gotta play hard to get if you want the shnook.

DEMETRIUS
I'll run from thee and hide me in the brakes,
And leave thee to the mercy of wild beasts.

HELENA
The wildest hath not such a heart as you.

(DEMETRIUS huffs out.)

HELENA
I'll follow thee and make a heaven of hell
To die upon the hand I love so well.

(HELENA runs after DEMETRIUS.)

ALL THREE STORYTELLERS
SHE'S GOT IT BAAAAAAD!!!

KAYTLIN
And that ain't good!

OBERON
Fare thee well, nymph! Ere he do leave this grove,
Thou shalt fly him, and he shall seek thy love.

(Enter PUCK.)

OBERON
Hast thou the flower there?

PUCK
Aye, there it is.

OBERON
I pray thee, give it me.

(PUCK gives him the flower.)

OBERON
I know a bank where the wild thyme blows.
Where oxlips and the nodding violet grows.
There sleeps Titania sometime of the night,
Lulled in these flowers with dances and delight.
And with the juice of this, I'll streak her eyes
And make her full of hateful fantasies.
(To PUCK.)
Take thou some of it, and seek through this grove.
A sweet Athenian lady who's in love

With a disdainful youth. Anoint *his* eyes,
But do it when the next thing he espies
May be the lady. Thou shalt know the man
By the Athenian garments he hath on.

JESSIE
Now THIS is important. Athenian garments. You know, a
kind of way they dress in a certain town...like Hackensack,
New Jersey...Poughkeepsie, New York...or...Athens,
Greece! Keep it in mind. You're gonna need it later on. For
the pop quiz. KIDDING!

PUCK
Fear not, my lord. Your servant shall do so.

(OBERON and PUCK exit in opposite directions.)

ANNA
Are we gonna have some fun now.

KAYTLIN
That herb Puck brought to Oberon has *some* flower power.

JESSIE
Squeeze it over someone's eyes when they're sleeping...
and when they wake...the first person...or dog...or box of
rocks they see...well, that's it! Lifetime commitment. In
love foreeeeever.

KAYTLIN
So Oberon...'cause he's a nice guy...

ANNA
Well, sometimes...

KAYTLIN
... is gonna help Helena out by getting Puck to squeeze it in Demetrius' eyes so he'll open them to Helena, and finally be madly in love with her.

JESSIE
And because Oberon ISN'T such a nice guy ...

ANNA
... sometimes ... he's got a trick up his sleeve about Titania. What do you think he's gonna do to her?
(She gets answers from the audience ... or doesn't.)
Don't make me come out there and drag you up here. *Whaddya think he's gonna do?*

(Someone is bound to shout: "Squeeze juice in TITANIA's eyes.")

JESSIE
On the nose!!!! Don't you wish this were "SO YOU WANT TO BE A MILLIONAIRE"?

(TITANIA and the FAIRIES dance out to flute music. They dance around TITANIA and lull her to sleep.)

COBWEB
Hence, away! Now all is well.
One aloof stand sentin-el.

(All the FAIRIES turn and point to one poor, lost soul ... the dim bulb of the group, whose name is MOTE. Then they leave. Left to guard the Queen ... MOTE tries his best ... but falls asleep almost immediately ... in sections ...

his ... head ... torso ... legs ... all collapsing quickly ... one after the other ... 'til he is out cold. OBERON enters and puts flower juice in TITANIA's eyes.)

OBERON
What thou seest when thou dost wake,
Do *it* for thy true love take.
Love and languish for his sake.
Be it lynx or cat or bear,
Pard or boar with bristled hair,
In thy eye what shall appear
When thou wak'st, it is thy dear.
Wake when some vile thing is near.

(OBERON exits.)

JESSIE *(making sounds like a submarine diving klaxon)*
TWO MORE RUNAWAY TEENS ON THE HORIZON!!!!

ANNA
The two who are running from her father, 'cause she won't marry Demetrius.

KAYTLIN
Hermia and Lysander ... remember?

JESSIE *(shouts offstage)*
Come on, guys. Ready for your close-up!

LYSANDER *(entering with HERMIA)*
We'll rest here, Hermia, if you think it good.

HERMIA
Be it so, Lysander. Find you out a bed,
For I upon this bank will rest my head.

(HERMIA lies down and immediately LYSANDER takes off his cloak, lies down beside her and spreads the cloak over them both.)

LYSANDER
One turf shall serve as pillow for us both;
One heart, one bed, one troth.

JESSIE
Well, well, well. Boys will be boys. But remember the old saying "Just say no"? Let's see if girls knew that in Shakespeare's day.

(HERMIA sits bolt upright and looks at LYSANDER.)

HERMIA
Nay, good Lysander. For my sake, my dear,
Lie Further Off. Do not lie so near.

KAYTLIN
Tell him, girl!!

LYSANDER *(as though hurt by this)*
Oh, take the sense, sweet, of my innocence!
I mean that my heart unto yours is knit,
So that but one heart we can make of it.

HERMIA
Lysander riddles very prettily.

Now much beshrew my manners and my pride
If Hermia meant to say Lysander lied.
But, gentle friend, for love and courtesy,
LIE...FURTHER...OFF!!!!!

LYSANDER *(leaping away, putting down his cloak a good
distance from her)*
Here is my bed. Sleep give thee all his rest.

ANNA
Well, that's settled. Smart girl. Now here comes old prank-
ster Puck.

KAYTLIN
Remember...he's looking for an Athenian teenage boy. Demetrius.

JESSIE
Hold the phone!! Lysander's got Athenian clothes on too!!!
Warn him off! Quick. Yell, "WRONG ATHENIAN! WRONG
ATHENIAN!" *(Submarine klaxon sound again)*

(The audience does so, or the girls harass them.)

PUCK
Through the forest have I gone,
But Athenian found I none.

(PUCK stumbles on LYSANDER.)

PUCK
Night and Silence!! Who is here?
Weeds of Athens he doth wear.

JESSIE
Weeds are Shakespeare for "clothes."

PUCK
Churl, upon thy eyes I throw
All the power this charm doth owe.

ANNA
Hold it!!!...Shout "NO" "NO." And then you'll be a rhymer like Shakespeare. Excuse me, Mr. Puck, could you say that line again, please?

PUCK
Churl, upon thy eyes I throw
All the power this charm doth owe...

AUDIENCE
No! No!

KAYTLIN
What a bunch of good playwrights you guys are!!!

(PUCK anoints LYSANDER's eyes anyway.)

JESSIE
I'll cover this territory ONE more time. Whoever gets a blast of flower power in the eyes, will fall in love with the next hunk of whatever living thing they see.

(Enter HELENA and DEMETRIUS.)

HELENA
Stay, though thou kill me, sweet Demetrius.

DEMETRIUS
Stay! I alone will go!

(DEMETRIUS exits.)

HELENA *(weeping)*
I am as ugly as a bear.
(She sees LYSANDER.)
But who is here? Lysander, on the ground.
If you live, good sir, awake.

LYSANDER *(waking, seeing HELENA)*
And run through fire I will for thy sweet sake.
Helena!
Where is Demetrius? Oh, how fit a word
Is that vile name to perish on my sword.

KAYTLIN
We got us some for-sure trouble here. Wait'll Hermia wakes
up. She'll think she's havin' a midsummer night's nightmare.

HELENA *(shocked)*
Do not say so, Lysander, say not so.
What tho he love your Hermia? Lord, what tho.
Yet Hermia still loves you. Then be content.

LYSANDER
Content with Hermia? No, I do repent
The tedious minutes I, with her, have spent.
Not Hermia but Helena, I love.
Who will not change a raven for a dove?

HELENA
Wherefore was I to this keen mockery born?

When at your hands did I deserve such scorn?
Fare you well.

   (HELENA exits.)

LYSANDER *(seeing HERMIA, asleep)*
Hermia, sleep thou there,
And never mayst thou come Lysander near.
And, all my powers, address your love and might
To honor Helena and to be her knight.

   (LYSANDER runs after HELENA.)

JESSIE
Well, that was a turnaround, wasn't it??

   (HERMIA starts awake, as from a dream.)

HERMIA
Lysander! What, removed? Lysander, lord!!

ALL THREE STORYTELLERS
Uh-oh.

HERMIA
Speak, if you hear.
I swoon almost with fear.
No? Then I well perceive you are not nigh.
Either death, or you, I'll find immediately!

   (HERMIA exits.)

JESSIE
OK. Let's go to the videotape. All four teens are now running through the forest. One of them has been enchanted by Puck...

ANNA
...the *wrong* one...

KAYTLIN
...and all the fairies and the King of the Forest and the Queen of the Forest are flying around annoying each other...

JESSIE
And now...here come the workers to rehearse their little play for Theseus' wedding. We're approaching capacity.

(Enter BOTTOM, QUINCE, STARVELING, SNOUT, SNUG and FLUTE.)

BOTTOM
Are we all met?

QUINCE
Here's a marvels convenient place for our rehearsals. We will do it in action as we will do it before the Duke.

BOTTOM
Peter Quince?

QUINCE
What sayest thou, bully Bottom?

BOTTOM
There are things in this comedy of Pyramus and Thisbe that will never please. First, Pyramus must draw a sword to kill himself, which the ladies cannot abide. How answer you that?

STARVELING
I believe we must leave the killing out when all is done.

BOTTOM
Not a whit! Write me a prologue, and let the prologue seem to say we will do no harm with our swords, and that Pyramus is not killed indeed. And for the more better assurance, tell them that I, Pyramus, am not Pyramus, but Bottom the weaver. This will put them out of fear.

QUINCE
Well, we will have such a prologue.

SNOUT
Will not the ladies be afeared of the lion?

STARVELING
I fear it, I promise you.

BOTTOM
There is not a more fearful wildfowl than your lion living, and we ought to look to it.

SNOUT
Therefore another prologue must tell he is not a lion.

JESSIE
There's gonna be more prologue than play here.

BOTTOM
Nay, you must name his name, and half his face must be
seen through the lion's neck, and he himself must speak
through, saying...
(BOTTOM puts on a very high voice.)
... "If you think I come hither as a lion, it were pity of my
life. No, I am no such thing. I am a man as other men are."
And there indeed let him name his name and tell them
plainly he is Snug the joiner.

QUINCE *(slightly impatient)*
Well, it shall be so. Then there is another thing: we must
have a wall in the great chamber, for Pyramus and Thisbe,
says the story, did talk through the chink of a wall.

BOTTOM *(excited: he HAS the solution)*
Some man or other must present Wall, and let him hold his
fingers thus...
(He parts his index and middle fingers in a sideways V.)
... and through that cranny shall Pyramus and Thisbe whisper.

QUINCE
If that may be, then all is well.

ANNA
Aren't they the cutest? I love these guys. OK. Tinkers. Cof-
fee break is over. Places for rehearsal!

QUINCE
Pyramus, you begin. When you have spoken your speech,
enter into that brake, and so everyone according to his cue.

(PUCK enters, makes a circling gesture around himself, and we hear the tinkling bells, signaling that he's invisible to the tinkers.)

PUCK
What ... a play? I'll be an actor perhaps, if I see cause.

QUINCE
Speak, Pyramus. Thisbe, stand forth.

BOTTOM *(as PYRAMUS, grossly overacting)*
Thisbe, the flowers of odious savors sweet ...

QUINCE *(prompting from the script)*
Odors! Odors!

BOTTOM *(as PYRAMUS)*
... odors savors sweet.
So hath thy breath, my dearest Thisbe dear.
But hark, a voice! Stay thou but here a while,
And by and by, I will to thee appear.

(BOTTOM exits. PUCK chases after him.)

JESSIE
Puck's a little devil. He's gonna play a trick on Bottom. I'd bet my bottom dollar on it.

FLUTE
Must I speak now?

QUINCE
Ay, you must, for Pyramus goes but to see a noise that he heard and is to come again.

FLUTE
O!
(as THISBE)
As true as truest horse, that yet would never tire...

(Enter PUCK, dancing around BOTTOM, who now has the ears and facial whiskers and large teeth of a donkey.)

ANNA
That Puck's got a gag a minute, doesn't he? The head of a jackass!!!

(The TINKERS stand frozen and stare.)

QUINCE
O monstrous! O strange! We are haunted! Pray, masters, fly, masters! Help!

(They all bolt in different directions, screaming.)

PUCK *(leaping with excitement)*
I'll follow you. I'll lead you about a round,
Sometimes a horse I'll be, sometime a hound.

(PUCK exits.)

JESSIE
This is priceless! Bottom doesn't know he's an ass. I know one or two folks like that.

(As BOTTOM speaks, the actor playing him should work in a braying sound periodically.)

BOTTOM
Why do they run away? This is knavery of them to make me afeared.

(Enter SNOUT.)

SNOUT
O Bottom, thou art changed. What do I see on thee?

BOTTOM
What do you see?

(BOTTOM moves toward SNOUT; SNOUT flees. Enter QUINCE.)

QUINCE
Bless thee, Bottom, bless thee! Thou art translated!

(QUINCE runs off.)

BOTTOM
I see their knavery. This is to make an ass of me, to fright me, if they could. I will walk up and down here, and I will sing, that they shall hear I am not afraid.
(He sings in a bad tenor.)
"The ouzel cock, so black of hue,
With orange, tawny bill,
The throstle with his note so true,
The wren with little quill—"

TITANIA *(waking up)*
What angel wakes me from my flow'ry bed?

KAYTLIN
Oooooops! Remember, Oberon put the flower juice in Titania's eyes, so she would love the first thing she saw when she woke up. And here it is, folks: AN ASS!!!!!

TITANIA *(to BOTTOM)*
I pray thee, gentle mortal, sing again.
Mine ear is much enamored of thy note,
So is mine eye enthral-led to thy shape...

JESSIE
Love is blind, sure enough.

TITANIA
...to say, to swear, I love thee.

ANNA
She's bewitched!!!!

BOTTOM
Methinks, mistress, you should have little reason for that. And yet, to say the truth, reason and love keep little company together nowadays.

KAYTLIN
Some things never change.

TITANIA
Thou art as wise as thou art beautiful.
Out of this wood, do not desire to go.
I do love thee. Therefore, go with me.
I'll give thee fairies to attend on thee,
And they shall fetch thee jewels from the deep.

(The three STORYTELLERS clap once, and FAIRIES appear flashing their pinspot lights.)

ANNA
There's service for you.

TITANIA *(to the FAIRIES)*
Be kind and courteous to this gentleman.
Feed him with purple grapes, green figs and mulberries.

PEASEBLOSSOM
Hail, mortal!

COBWEB
Hail!

MUSTARDSEED
Hail!

MOTE
Hail!

TITANIA
Come, wait upon him. Lead him to my bower.

(They all exit.)

JESSIE *(rubbing her palms together)*
Alrighty. We got teenagers bewitched and crazy about the wrong person. The tinkers' rehearsal has hit a wall because one of them was turned into a jackass. And we got the Queen of the Fairies hoodwinked into LOVING that ass.

ANNA
And who's responsible for all this crazy, mixed-up mayhem?

(PUCK jumps out from the wings and gives a raspberry, then leaps about laughing.)

KAYTLIN
That's right…the class clown. Just like in class, right? Art imitating life.

(PUCK leaps about the three STORYTELLERS and does a Three Stooges' noise. OBERON walks on and PUCK grabs him. In mime, walking around, PUCK tells OBERON of all his antics.)

JESSIE
So he tells his boss all about it.

PUCK
…when in that moment, so it came to pass
Titania woke and straightway loved an ass!!

(They both howl with laughter.)

OBERON
This falls out better than I could devise.
But hast thou yet latched the Athenian's eyes
With the love juice, as I did bid thee do?

(PUCK nods "yes," vigorously. DEMETRIUS and HER-MIA enter.)

OBERON
Stand close. This is the same Athenian.

PUCK *(looking guilty)*
This is the woman, but not this the man.

(OBERON puts hands on hips and gives him a "slow-burn" turn. PUCK and OBERON hide behind the trees.)

DEMETRIUS
O, why rebuke you him who loves you so?

HERMIA
If thou hast slain Lysander in his sleep,
Then kill me too.
Would he have stolen away
From sleeping Hermia?
It cannot be but thou hast murdered him.
Ah, good Demetrius, wilt thou give him me?

DEMETRIUS
I would rather give his carcass to my hounds.

HERMIA
Out, dog! Out, cur! Hast thou slain him, then?

DEMETRIUS
I am not guilty of Lysander's blood
Nor is he dead for aught that I can tell.

HERMIA
See me no more, whether he be dead or no.

(He runs off.)

DEMETRIUS
There is no following her in this fierce vein.
Here, therefore, for a while I will remain.

(He lies down and immediately falls asleep)

OBERON *(angrily, to PUCK)*
What hast thou done? Thou hast mistaken quite
And laid the love juice on some true love's sight!

(PUCK cringes at OBERON's anger.)

OBERON
About the wood go swifter than the wind
And Helena of Athens look thou find.
By some illusion, see thou bring her here.
I'll charm his eyes against she do appear.

PUCK
I go, I go, look how I go.

(PUCK runs offstage, and OBERON immediately puts the love juice in DEMETRIUS' eyes. Instantly, PUCK runs back on.)

PUCK
Captain of our fairy band,
Helena is here at hand,
And the youth mistook by me,
Pleading for a lover's fee.
Shall we their fond pageant see?
Lord, what fools these mortals be!

JESSIE
Got that right.

OBERON
Stand aside. The noise they make
Will cause Demetrius to awake.

(Enter HELENA pursued by LYSANDER.)

LYSANDER
Why should you think that I should woo in scorn?

HELENA
These vows are Hermia's. Will you give her o'er?

LYSANDER
I had no judgment when to her I swore.

HELENA
Nor none, in my mind, now you give her o'er.

KAYTLIN
That's tellin' him, girlfriend!

LYSANDER
Demetrius loves her and he loves not you.

(DEMETRIUS wakes up and sees HELENA.

DEMETRIUS
O, Helen, goddess, nymph, perfect, divine!

ANNA
I guess a leopard CAN change his spots.

HELENA
O Spite! O Hell! I see you all are bent
To set against me for your merriment.

LYSANDER
You are unkind, Demetrius. Be not so,
For you love Hermia; this you know, I know.
And here, with all goodwill, with all my heart,
In Hermia's love, I yield you up my part.

DEMETRIUS
Lysander, keep thy Hermia. I will none.
If e'er I loved her, all that love is gone.

LYSANDER
Helen, it is not so.

(HERMIA enters. Stares at LYSANDER, then speaks.)

HERMIA
Why unkindly didst thou leave me so?

LYSANDER
Why should he stay whom love doth press to go?

HERMIA
What love could press Lysander from my side?

LYSANDER
Why, fair Helena!
(To HERMIA.)
Why seek'st thou me? Could not this make thee know,
The hate I bear thee made me leave thee so?

HERMIA
You speak not as you think. It cannot be.

HELENA
Lo, *she* is one of this confederacy!
Injurious Hermia! Will you join with men
In scorning your poor friend?

HERMIA
I scorn you not. It seems that you scorn me.

HELENA
Fare you well.

LYSANDER
Stay, gentle Helena.
My love, my life, my soul, fair Helena.

HELENA
O excellent!!

HERMIA *(to LYSANDER)*
Sweet, do not scorn her so.

LYSANDER
Helen, I love thee. By my life, I do.

DEMETRIUS
I say I love thee more than he can do.

LYSANDER *(holding up his fists)*
If thou say so, withdraw and prove it too.

DEMETRIUS
Quick! Come!!

JESSIE
Call 911! Fight! Fight!!

(HERMIA throws herself on LYSANDER and won't let go.)

LYSANDER
Hang off, thou cat, thou burr! Vile thing, let loose,
Or I will shake thee from me like a serpent.

HERMIA
Do you not jest?
Am I not Hermia? Are not you Lysander?
Since night you loved me ...
(She thinks about that.)
... yet since night, you left me.
Why then you left me— O, the gods forbid—
In earnest, shall I say?

LYSANDER
Ay, by my life
I do hate thee and love Helena.

ALL THREE STORYTELLERS
Harsh!!!

(HERMIA lets go of LYSANDER and turns on HELENA.)

HERMIA
You thief of love! What, have you come by night
And stolen my love's heart from him?

HELENA
What, will you tear

Impatient answers from my gentle tongue?
Fie, fie, you counterfeit, you puppet, you!

JESSIE
Anyone reached 911 yet? CATFIGHT!!!!!!

HERMIA
"Puppet"? Why so? Ay, that way goes the game.
Now I perceive that she hath made compare
Between our statures; she hath urged her height,
And with her personage, her *tall* personage,
Her *height*, forsooth, she hath prevailed with him.
How low am I, thou painted maypole? Speak!
How low am I? I am not yet so low
But that my nails can reach unto thine eyes.

   (KAYTLIN blows a whistle.)

KAYTLIN
Dive! Dive!

   *(JESSIE offers the klaxon sound effect. HERMIA chases
   HELENA around the stage with the boys trying to catch
   them. It should be rather Keystone Cops-ish. DEMETRIUS
   and LYSANDER finally hold HERMIA off of HELENA. If
   the actress is short enough, they could hold her off the
   ground and let her kick.)*

HELENA
Let her not strike me! You perhaps may think,
Because she is something lower than myself
That I can match her.

HERMIA
"Lower." Hark, again!

LYSANDER
Be not afraid. She shall not harm thee, Helena.

HELENA
O, when she is angry, she is keen and shrewd.
She was a vixen when she went to school,
And tho she be but little, she is fierce.

HERMIA
"Little" again? Nothing but "low" and "little"?
(straining to get her hands on HELENA)
Let me come to her.

LYSANDER
Get you gone, you dwarf, you acorn.

DEMETRIUS *(to LYSANDER)*
Speak not for Helena. Take not her part.

(The two MEN drop HERMIA and face each other nose to nose.)

LYSANDER
Now follow, if thou darest.

(They exit slowly, circling each other with fists threatening...in a big, deliberate circle. HELENA starts backing away from HERMIA.)

HERMIA
Nay, go not back.

HELENA
Your hands than mine are quicker for a fray.
My legs are longer though, to run away.

(HELENA dashes off with HERMIA in hot pursuit. OBERON comes out of hiding with PUCK.)

OBERON
This is thy negligence.

PUCK
Believe me, King of Shadows, I mistook.
Did not you tell me I should know the man
By the Athenian garments he had on?

(OBERON grabs PUCK, walks him around, and tells him what he has to do).

ANNA
So Oberon tells Puck to lead the teens on a merry chase through the woods...

(LYSANDER and DEMETRIUS enter from opposite sides of the stage ... backs to each other ... creeping backwards ... toward center ... until they almost collide ... but don't ... circling around each other ... never actually seeing each other ... and creep off to the wings. Then HELENA dashes on ... at full tilt ... HERMIA ... hot on her heels ... they exit ... one after the other.)

KAYTLIN
... until they're all so tired, they fall down and sleep.

(We watch a wild run through the forest, PUCK leading one and then the other to chase his shadow. He makes noises which make DEMETRIUS think he's on the trail of LYSANDER and vice versa. The same with the GIRLS. They finally all fall down into a deep sleep, just a tree or two away from each other.)

OBERON
Now, crush this herb into Lysander's eye.
(He gives the magic herb to PUCK.)
When they next wake, all this derision
Shall seem a dream.
I'll to my Queen and will her charm-ed eye release
From monster's view, and all things shall be peace.

(PUCK applies the nectar to LYSANDER's eyes.)

PUCK *(to LYSANDER)*
When thou wakest,
Thou takest
True delight
In the sight
Of thy former lady's eye.

(PUCK rolls LYSANDER and HERMIA so they are facing each other and no mistakes can happen. He does the same with DEMETRIUS and HELENA, just to be sure).

PUCK
Jack shall have Jill
Naught shall be ill.

KAYTLIN
Jack and Jill. So *this* is where that comes from.

JESSIE
But now Oberon's gotta lift the spell off Titania...so she
won't be doting on an ass.

*(We see TITANIA and BOTTOM dancing with FAIRIES
around them. She kisses his ass face. OBERON watches.
Then to PUCK:)*

OBERON
Her dotage now I do begin to pity.
I will undo this hateful imperfection of her eyes.
And, gentle Puck, take this scalp
From off the head of this Athenian swain.
I will release the Fairy Queen.

*(TITANIA and BOTTOM lie down to sleep. OBERON ap-
plies the nectar to her eyes.)*

OBERON
Now, my Titania, wake you, my sweet Queen.

TITANIA *(waking and seeing OBERON)*
My Oberon, what visions have I seen!
Methought I was enamored of an ass.

OBERON
There lies your love.

TITANIA
O, how mine eyes do loathe his visage now!

PUCK *(removing the ass head from BOTTOM)*
Now, when thou wakest, with thine own fool's eyes peep.

OBERON
Sound music!
Now thou and I are new in amity,
And will tomorrow midnight, solemnly
Dance in Duke Theseus' house triumphantly.
There shall the pairs of faithful lovers be
Wedded, with Theseus, all in jollity.

JESSIE
As if the forest wasn't crowded enough, guess who else is
here all of a sudden. Duke Theseus, his fiancée Hyppolyta,
and of course the other grownup...Hermia's dad, Egeus.
(To the other two STORYTELLERS.)
Well, come on, girls. Time to grow up. We play these guys,
remember?

KAYTLIN
Oh, yeah. "Growing old ain't for sissies."

   *(They all put on their grown-up hats. They walk around
   a minute and then stumble on HERMIA.)*

JESSIE *(as THESEUS)*
Soft, what nymphs are these?

ANNA *(as EGEUS)*
My lord, this is my daughter here asleep,
And this Lysander; this Demetrius is,
This Helena.
I wonder of their being here together.

JESSIE *(as THESEUS)*
Is not this the day
That Hermia should give answer of her choice?

ANNA *(as EGEUS)*
It is, my lord.

*(JESSIE comes out of character, becoming the STORY-
TELLER.)*

JESSIE *(to the audience)*
Remember this? Her choices are to marry Demetrius, become a nun, or die. Some horse race, huh? Let's see what
she does.

KAYTLIN
Well, hold it just a sec.

JESSIE
You're supposed to be Hyppolyta in this scene.

KAYTLIN
She doesn't have enough lines for my taste. I got an idea.
(To the audience.) What do you think she ought to do? All
those in favor of her marrying Demetrius...applaud. All in
favor of her becoming a nun...let's hear from YOU. OK...
All in favor of her dying?
(If anyone applauds, she says:)
I don't wanna be on a desert island with you!! *(She cocks
her ear toward the audience.)* What's that you say? MARRY
LYSANDER???? The grownups are dead against it. And you
know how they are when their minds are made up.

JESSIE
Yeah. I was grounded for most of 7th grade.

ANNA
More information than we need, Jess.

(She goes back to being EGEUS.)

JESSIE *(as THESEUS)*
I pray you all, stand up.

(The TEENS jump to their feet. They're each facing their right partner and look lovingly at their true loves.)

JESSIE *(as THESEUS)*
I know you two are rival enemies.
How comes this gentle concord?

LYSANDER
My lord, I shall reply amazedly,
Half sleep, half-waking.
And now I do bethink me, so it is:
I came with Hermia hither. Our intent
Was to be gone from Athens.

ANNA *(as EGEUS)*
Enough, enough. —My lord, you have enough.
I beg the law, the law, upon his head.
They would have stolen away—they would,
Demetrius.

DEMETRIUS
My lord, I know not by what power

(But by some power it is) my love to Hermia
Melted as the snow.
The object and the pleasure of mine eye,
Is only Helena.

(ANNA as EGEUS begins to huff and puff and walk around in a dither.)

JESSIE *(breaking out of THESEUS)*
What are you doing?

ANNA *(as EGEUS)*
Protesting my grown-up, parental, I've-lived-a-long-time-so-I-know-better-than-you RIGHTS!!!!!!

JESSIE
Except I'm the grownup that's gonna trump your ace here.
I knew I liked this role.
(as THESEUS)
Fair lovers you are fortunately met.
Egeus, I will overbear your will,
For in the temple, by and by, with us,
These couples shall eternally be knit.
Come, Hippolyta.

(Exit THESEUS, HIPPOLYTA and EGEUS. The three STORYTELLERS come right back on in their regular hats.)

KAYTLIN
I hate multiple casting. It's sooooo much work.

JESSIE
Which is why they pay us the big bucks.

DEMETRIUS *(to the other three TEENS)*
Are you sure that we are awake? It seems to me
That yet we sleep, we dream. Do not you think
The Duke was here and bid us follow him?

HERMIA
Yea, and my father.

HELENA
And Hippolyta.

LYSANDER
And he did bid us follow to the temple.

DEMETRIUS
Why, then, we are awake. Let's follow him,
And by the way, let us recount our dreams.

(The LOVERS skip off after THESEUS.)

ANNA
So much for the teens. So much for the fairies. We only
have left...

ALL THREE STORYTELLERS
The Rude Mechanicals...

JESSIE
The star of their little play became an ass, as you recall,
thanks to Mr. Puck...class clown extraordinaire!!!

KAYTLIN
But here he is...Bottom...waking up from his midsummer
night's dream.

BOTTOM *(starting awake)*
When my cue comes, call me, and I will answer.
(He stares around for a moment.)
God's my life! I have had a most rare vision. I have had a
dream past the wit of man to say what dream it was. Man
is but an ass if he go about to expound his dream. I will get
Peter Quince to write a ballad of this dream. It shall be
called *Bottom's Dream* because it hath no bottom. And I
will sing it in the latter end of the play, before the Duke.

(BOTTOM exits.)

KAYTLIN
So everybody's all married up to who they should be married up to, and now they're gonna have a little reception
with entertainment. So we have to play the grownups, remember? I'm the girl grown up.

(She flips her hair back at ANNA and JESSIE.)

JESSIE
Just wait'll the next play, sweetie.

*(Enter the four TEENS, joined by the three STORYTELL-
ERS as the grownups.)*

KAYTLIN *(as HIPPOLYTA)*
'Tis strange, my Theseus, what these lovers speak of.

JESSIE *(as THESEUS)*
Lovers and madmen have such seething brains.
Come now, is there no play?

KAYTLIN *(as HIPPOLYTA, hands him a long scroll)*
Here, mighty Theseus.

JESSIE *(as THESEUS, reads aloud from the list)*
"The Battle With the Centaurs, to Be Sung
By an Athenian Eunuch to the Harp."
We'll none of that.
"A Tedious Brief Scene of Young Pyramus
And His Love Thisbe, Very Tragical Mirth."
(He looks up from the scroll.)
"Merry" and "Tragical"? "Tedious" and "Brief"?
That is hot ice and wondrous strange snow!

KAYTLIN *(as HIPPOLYTA)*
A play there is, my lord, some ten words long,
Which is as brief as I have known a play,
But by ten words, I hear it is too long.

JESSIE *(as THESEUS)*
We will hear it.

*(He claps his hands smartly. QUINCE, as PROLOGUE,
enters, shyly, looking around at the great palace.)*

QUINCE *(as PROLOGUE)*
If we offend, it is with our goodwill.
That you should think we come not to offend...
But with goodwill.

(PROLOGUE scurries off to the wings.)

LYSANDER
He hath rid his prologue like a rough colt.

JESSIE *(as THESEUS)*
Who's next?

(Enter BOTTOM, FLUTE, SNOUT, STARVELING, SNUG and QUINCE.)

QUINCE *(as PROLOGUE)*
Gentles, perchance you wonder at this show.
This man is Pyramus, if you would know.
This beauteous lady Thisbe is certain.
This man with lime and roughcast doth present
"Wall," that vile wall which did these lovers sunder;
And through Wall's chink, poor souls, they are content
To whisper.

(As the STORYTELLERS do the following, QUINCE continues to bring each of the characters forward, as they are named by the STORYTELLERS. He mouths words as though he is talking.)

JESSIE *(changing from THESEUS)*
And so he rambles on and on, 'til the married couples are about to doze. He introduces all the guys: Starveling is "Moonshine," Snug is "Lion," etc., etc.

ANNA *(changing from EGEUS)*
Well these little guys have never gotten to speak to royalty. They have LOTS to say. Like going to the White House for a one-on-one.

KAYTLIN *(changing from HIPPOLYTA)*
He tells them the whole plot...before they even see it. That
Pyramus and Thisbe decide to meet at Ninus' tomb by moon-
light.

JESSIE
That a lion intercepts Thisbe, scares her off, she drops her
cape, and the lion puts his bloody mouth on it. When Pyramus sees the cape, he thinks she's dead and kills himself.
It's really a tragedy.

ANNA
But the way these guys go at it...it's pretty funny. As in
"Merry" AND "Tragical." No false advertising here.

JESSIE *(switching her hat to THESEUS)*
Pyramus draws near the wall. Silence.

BOTTOM *(as PYRAMUS)*
O night, which ever art when day is not!
I fear my Thisbe's promise is forgot.
Thou wall, O wall, O sweet and lovely wall...
*(BOTTOM kisses the wall and SNOUT smacks him on the
nose.)*
Show me thy chink to blink through with mine eyne.
(SNOUT spreads his fingers in a V.)
Thanks, courteous wall.
(He looks through the chink.)
But what see I? No Thisbe do I see.
O wicked wall, through whom I see no bliss,
Cursed be thy stones for thus deceiving me!

(BOTTOM smacks SNOUT on the arm.)

JESSIE *(as THESEUS)*
The wall, methinks, being sensible, should curse again.

BOTTOM *(out of his character, speaking to THESEUS)*
No, in truth, sir, he should not. "Deceiving me" is Thisbe's
cue. She is to enter now, and I am to spy her through the wall.
You shall see it will fall pat as I told you. Yonder she comes.

(Enter FLUTE as THISBE.)

FLUTE *(as THISBE)*
O wall, full often hast thou heard my moans,
My cherry lips have often kissed thy stones.

(She kisses the wall, and SNOUT giggles, embarrassed.)

BOTTOM *(as PYRAMUS)*
I see a voice! Now will I to the chink
To spy and I can hear my Thisbe's face.
Thisbe?

FLUTE *(as THISBE)*
My love! Thou art my love, I think.

BOTTOM *(as PYRAMUS)*
O kiss me through the hole of this vile wall.

*(They both lean in to kiss, but SNOUT...whose arm is
falling asleep...has moved it to shake up the circulation...
and they kiss the arm instead.)*

FLUTE *(as THISBE)*
I kiss the wall's hole...not your lips at all.

BOTTOM *(as PYRAMUS)*
Will thou at Ninny's tomb meet me straightway?

FLUTE *(as THISBE)*
I come without delay.

(BOTTOM and FLUTE exit.)

SNOUT *(as WALL)*
Thus have I, Wall, my part discharg-ed so,
And, being done, thus Wall away doth go.

(He exits, slowly, looking longingly back at his moment of glory.)

KAYTLIN *(as HIPPOLYTA)*
This is the silliest stuff that ever I heard.

JESSIE *(as THESEUS)*
Here come two noble beasts in, a man and a lion.

(Enter SNUG as LION, and STARVELING as MOON-SHINE.)

SNUG *(as LION)*
You, ladies, you whose gentle hearts do fear
The smallest monstrous mouse that creeps on floor,
May now perchance both quake and tremble here,
When lion rough in wildest rage doth roar.
(He gives a sweet roar.)

JESSIE *(as THESEUS)*
A very gentle beast and of a good conscience.

STARVELING *(as MOON, holding a lantern)*
This lantern doth the horn-ed moon present.
Myself the man in the moon, do seem to be.

DEMETRIUS
Silence. Here comes Thisbe.

(Enter FLUTE, as THISBE.)

FLUTE *(as THISBE)*
This is old Ninny's tomb. Where is my love?

(The LION roars, THISBE runs off, dropping her cape.)

DEMETRIUS
Well roared, Lion.

JESSIE *(as THESEUS)*
Well run, Thisbe.

(The LION worries the cape with his teeth.)

LYSANDER
Well moused, Lion.

(BOTTOM as PYRAMUS enters.)

BOTTOM *(as PYRAMUS)*
What dreadful dole is here!
O dainty duck! O dear!
(He picks up the bloodstained cape.)
What, stained with blood?

Come tears, confound!
Out sword, and wound!
(PYRAMUS stabs himself. He proceeds to have a long, agonizing, rolling-around death.)
Thus die I, thus, thus, thus.
Now am I dead.
Now am I fled;
Tongue, lose thy light!
Moon, take thy flight.

> *(MOONSHINE starts to leave but comes back to make sure BOTTOM is all right. BOTTOM waves him out sharply. He flees.)*

BOTTOM *(as PYRAMUS)*
Now die, die, die, die, die.

> *(PYRAMUS FINALLY dies. THISBE enters.)*

FLUTE *(as THISBE)*
O Pyramus, arise!
Dead? Dead?
Tongue, not a word.
Come, trusty sword,
Come, blade, my breast imbrue!
(THISBE stabs herself.)
And farewell, friends.
(Waving to THESEUS and all the ROYAL COURT. Perhaps a smidge too long.)
Thus Thisbe ends.
Adieu, adieu, adieu.

(THISBE dies. BOTTOM leaps up from the dead.)

BOTTOM
Will it please you to see the epilogue?

JESSIE *(as THESEUS)*
No epilogue, I pray you. For your play needs no excuse.

(Music begins and all dance—FAIRIES, TINKERS, ROYAL COURT. The dance ends. Perhaps we hear a clock toll midnight.)

JESSIE *(as THESEUS)*
The iron tongue of midnight hath told twelve. Lovers to bed!

(All start to leave; STORYTELLERS switch hats, back to storytellers; the FAIRIES remain, swaying with their pinspot flashlights.)

OBERON
Through the house give glimmering light,
Every elf and fairy sprite.

TITANIA
Hand in hand, with fairy grace,
Will we sing and bless this place.

(They all scatter to the wings. PUCK comes to the lip of the stage. To the audience:)

PUCK
If we shadows have offended,
Think but this and all is mended:

That you have but slumbered here
While these visions did appear.
And this weak and idle theme,
No more yielding but a dream,
Gentles, do not reprehend.
If you pardon, we will mend.
And as I am an honest Puck,
If we have unearn-ed luck
Now to scape the serpent's tongue,
We will make amends ere long.
Else the Puck a liar call
So goodnight unto you all.
Give me your hands if we be friends,
And Robin shall restore amends.

(Lights go out and come up again full on an empty stage. The three STORYTELLERS emerge to take a bow together. JESSIE steps forward. To the audience:)

JESSIE
OK. Pop quiz. For the test, don't'cha know. Shout out the names.

(She points to ANNA, who bows. The audience shouts EGEUS! She then points to KAYTLIN who bows. The audience shouts HIPPOLYTA! She bows herself, the audience shouts THESEUS! As each of the characters comes out, the STORYTELLERS urge, harass the audience. And help them where necessary. Finally, a full company bow.)

THE END

COSTUMES

Budgetary concerns worked to our benefit in the design of the costumes. Since our budget was more of the "virtual" realm than the "real" one, we were required to exercise our imaginations to produce low cost/free costumes. Thrift stores and garage sales yielded a rich harvest of wild and inexpensive costume pieces, but due to the uncertain nature of the "stock," we recommend that the costumer start shopping early and plan to make several trips in order to accumulate a wide selection of costume pieces. This type of preparation enabled us to avoid having to construct any of the costumes.

Our storytellers presented a costuming challenge since they also had parts as Shakespearean characters. This duality challenge was met by costuming the storytellers in typical school wear and providing them with handmade top-hat-style hats made of felt. One side of each hat was decorated with a bright, carnival-style mask. The other side was decorated with a mask of a famous adult. As the storytellers moved in and out of their dual roles, they had only to turn their hats around to signal the change in character.

Costuming the various fairies was done with thrift store negligees enhanced with silk flowers. They wore headbands and matching wristbands decorated with silk flowers. To maintain a more ethereal appearance than bare feet communicate, we put inexpensive ballet slippers on the fairies. As the Queen of the Fairies, Titania was provided the prettiest of the peignoir sets and a tiara.

We looked for colorful African print and tie-dyed balloon-style pants to pair with bare chests and suspenders for our male forest spirits. Their leader, Oberon, carried out the bare-chested theme without a tie, but maintained a kingly presence garbed in a wool bathrobe trimmed with decorative braid over a pair of colorful balloon pants. Puck's costume is the same as the other male spirits with the addition of a porkpie hat and bow tie. Boys uncomfortable with being bare-chested could certainly wear T-shirts.

Our Rude Mechanicals became "Rude Mechanics" and were fitted with safety helmets, lab coats and clipboards. The back of the lab coats were decorated with computer-generated iron-on logos reading "Rude Mechanics" and each wore a large number on the front of his lab coat instead of a name tag. When Bottom was transformed into an ass, he was fitted with a set of Easter bunny ears attached to a headband, some large teeth, and whiskers. Since hardhats and lab coats are not always readily found at no or low cost, considerations for other costumes could include overalls or coveralls and safety goggles, or "normal" teenaged male clothing with multiple toy cell phones and pagers attached to a tool belt.

Other Shakespearean characters were robed in toga-like shifts constructed of old bed linens of various colors and patterns and tied with belts made of tasseled drapery ties, but in the absence of such a fortuitous find, any type of belting, including recycled men's ties, can be used.

PROPS

pinspot flashlights (for as many fairies as you cast)
sprig of herbs (plastic will do)
5 small manuscripts (for the rude mechanicals)
1 large manuscript (for Peter Quince)
1 scroll from which Thesus reads the names of the plays
1 lantern (moon)
1 cape (Thisbe)
materials to make an ass head (ears, whiskers, teeth)
bells to ring for invisibility of Oberon and Puck
whistle for storyteller
bell tolling midnight
crash box (backstage, to introduce the Rude Mechanicals)

DIRECTOR'S NOTES

DIRECTOR'S NOTES